Good luck and good
bananas.

J. Blazing

What people are saying about
SMALL BUSINESS IS LIKE A BUNCH OF BANANAS

ENTREPRENEURS!! This book will entertain, uplift, and help you strip away doubts, fears, and negative beliefs. You'll have fun while picking up lots of practical wisdom.

Chérie Carter-Scott, Ph.D.
Bestselling author of *If Life is a Game, These are the Rules*
and *If Success is a Game, These are the Rules*

Wow! Jim Blasingame has really captured the essence of the entrepreneurial spirit. This book should be required reading for every small business owner and wannabe.

Russell Brown
Author of *Strategies for Successfully Buying or Selling a Business*

Jim Blasingame's book provides huge helpings of the fortitude and faith it takes to succeed as a small business owner. His perspective, spiced with the collective wisdom of many other brilliant people, is a perfect dose of inspiration and reality so necessary to small business owners, who often lack someone to turn to. And you can write that on a rock!

Mary Westheimer
CEO, BookZone, Inc.

Jim has been a tireless advocate for small businesses. In this inspiring book he gives us what we all need to carry on in times of fear and hopelessness—wisdom and encouragement to follow our dreams and our hearts.

Joseph Bailey, M.A.
Author of *The Speed Trap;* and *Slowing Down to the Speed of Life*

Jim Blasingame has given small business owners something unique—secret recipes on how to gain and maintain the attitude necessary for success.

Barbara Weltman, Esq.
Author of *The Complete Idiot's Guide to Starting a Home-Based Business*

"Small Business is Like a Bunch of Bananas" is the "Chicken Soup" for small business. It is so full of encouragements, wisdom, and humor to get you through an entrepreneurial day that it should be on the desk of every small business owner.

Beverley Williams
President and Founder, American Association Of Home-Based Businesses

Over the 35 years of practicing law in Washington, D.C., I have been searching for a book for my small business clients that will help them make wise decisions, particularly at their toughest times. At last, Jim Blasingame has given us just that book. My new advice to clients: Read this gem of a book, then come see me.

John O. Fox, Esq.
Author of *If Americans Really Understood the Income Tax*

I have known Jim Blasingame for several years and he's one of the good guys. This man walks the talk and cares passionately about what he does and the people he serves. Jim is a man of integrity, truth and commitment, and these qualities shine through in his work on radio and in this book. He's a man you can always learn from—I have!

Azriela Jaffe
Author of *Create Your Own Luck* (Adams Media 2000)

Like any good banana, Jim Blasingame's book is enjoyable to consume, easy to digest, and quickly turns into energy for entrepreneurs. This book is required reading for any savvy business owner.

Jeff Zbar
2001 Small Business Journalist of the Year, and Author of *Safe@Home*

Jim Blasingame knows small business because he has lived it. In this book, Jim's timely and thoughtful advice speaks to the heart and mind of the entrepreneur— the backbone of American economic life.

Burton W. Folsom, Jr., Ph.D.
Historian in Residence, Center for the American Idea
Author of *The Myth Of The Robber Barons;* and *Empire Builders*

Jim's book is warm, witty, and filled with encouraging and uplifting messages to cheer you on. His words become your guide and mentor on the path to small business success and entrepreneurial greatness. THIS BOOK SHOULD BE ON EVERY BUSINESS OWNER'S DESK!

Jim Donovan
Author of *This is Your Life, Not a Dress Rehearsal*

Wow!!! Lots of great bits of advice in bunches, just like bananas. You can make tasty mental snacks out of these profit-making tidbits. This book is like Jim's show, filled with great ideas, encouragement, and information. Buy a couple of dozen for your friends in business.

Wally Bock
Digital Age Strategy Guru; Publisher of *Monday Memo*

Jim Blasingame's book is a splendid collection of sound advice for anyone running a business. They all are presented in a lively, straightforward and succinct way that will make reading this book easy, inviting, and profitable.

Gary Shilling, Ph.D.
President, A. Gary Shilling & Co., Inc.
Author of *Deflation*; and *FORBES* columnist

Jim Blasingame has packed a lot of wisdom in this small package—there is a thoughtful and life-changing idea on virtually every page.

Eugene Griessman
Author of *The Words Lincoln Lived By;* and
Time Tactics of Very Successful People

In this book, Jim Blasingame tells us how to leverage the good times and deal with the tough moments—solid advice for small business owners, and all based on proven evidence.

Robert Dilenschneider
President, The Dilenschneider Group; and Author of *Moses:CEO*

Sparkling. Delightful. Educational. Jim's book is guidance from a pioneer for pioneers. A thought provoking feast, overflowing with uncommon common sense and inspiration. I especially like the poem—a nice surprise.

Steven C. Martin
President, Business Solutions—The Positive Way

Jim Blasingame speaks to the entrepreneur in all of us. His sage advice and wit provide wonderful guidance on how to approach both the challenges and opportunities that make business—and life—so interesting, demanding, and ultimately rewarding. Wisdom is seldom found in such a friendly and compassionate package. Thanks Jim.

Charles W. Kadlec
Managing Director, J. & W. Seligman & Co. Inc.
Author of *Dow 100,000: Fact or Fiction*

This book ought to be required reading for everybody even thinking about starting or running a business, and it would do a lot of good in the business schools, too. Jim is a fixture on my web radio dial because of his common sense, plain talk, and real-world wisdom. Jim's book is everything I expected of him and more. Read it and keep it on your desk.

Tim Berry
President, Palo Alto Software

Jim Blasingame

SMALL BUSINESS
IS LIKE A
BUNCH OF BANANAS
You Have to Remove the Peels
to Get to the Good Stuff!

SBN
BOOKS

Small Business Is Like A Bunch Of Bananas
You Have to Remove the Peels to Get to the Good Stuff!

Publisher's Cataloging-In-Publication
(Provided by Quality Books, Inc.)

Blasingame, Jim.
    Small business is like a bunch of bananas : you have to remove the peels to get to the good stuff! / Jim Blasingame. — 1st ed.
    p. cm.
    Includes bibliographical references.
    LCCN: 2001088007
    ISBN: 0-9709278-0-0

    1. Small business—Management. 2. Entrepreneurship.
I. Title.

HD62.7.B53 2001   658.02'2
                                     QBI01-200578

10 9 8 7 6 5 4 3 2 1

This book is dedicated to my parents,
James and Virginia,
to whom I am grateful for many things,
but especially for loving me enough
to teach me how to work.

TABLE OF CONTENTS

ACKNOWLEDGMENTS

Behind every successful project there is always one person without whose contribution there would be no project—someone who works behind the scenes as the cheerleader, psychologist, critic, and safe harbor. I am daily grateful to have such a person in my business and in my life. Davonna, this book is as much yours as it is mine.

To Jim O'Brien, thanks for believing in me.

To the crew at A. Tomlinson-Sims, who put their professional touch on this book—thanks for your contribution, encouragement, and energy.

Thanks to Lindsey Stricklin, Tony Stubbs, and Don Sadler, for their excellent editing, and to Burt Folsom, my resident historian.

I must also take this opportunity to thank my teachers and professors. Special thanks to those who tried to teach me English composition, especially my first and last, Marilyn Moore and J. Nicholas Winn, III. I regret that I can't list all of your names here, but what I really regret is that I won't be able to see the incredulity on your faces when you receive your complimentary copy of a book by Jim Blasingame. Please try to resist the urge to use a red pen.

Some of the great blessings in my life are the relationships I have acquired with the hundreds of members of my Brain Trust—the experts who join me on my talk show. We truly have created a community of people who strive for and encourage excellence, and all have contributed in some way to the creation of this book.

There are certain members of The Brain Trust whom I would like to identify and thank for their specific contribution: Grace-Marie Arnett, Karen Kerrigan, Burt Folsom, Mary Westheimer, Steve Martin, Dan Poynter, Marc Allen, Russell Brown, Jim Donovan, Azriela Jaffe, Tim Berry, Barbara Weltman, Ivan Misner, and Andrew Sherman. Thanks for always being there when I needed an ear, a critical eye, or a valuable opinion.

There is an ancient saying that goes something like this: *If on the day you die you can name one good friend for each of the fingers on just one hand, you will die a rich man.* I am not yet ready to go, but my Brain Trust alone has already made me rich.

And, finally, to paraphrase Winston Churchill, I want to thank the few who do so much for so many: small business owners. Your commitment, courage, and spirit continue to inspire me. You are my heroes.

FOREWORD

When I think of entrepreneurs, I first think of their vision, tenacity, and creativity, but especially, I think of their courage.

Small business owners face many obstacles as they carve out their niche in the marketplace—obstacles such as competition and raising the capital needed to grow. Not to mention litigious lawyers, and onerous and oft-unfathomable government rules and taxes. These certainly are speed bumps on the small business highway, but they are, after all, just challenges that all businesses have to manage.

For entrepreneurs, the prime challenge is being able to reach inside themselves to find the courage and inspiration they need to face the marketplace, typically alone, and often in the face of negativism from non-entrepreneurs.

If I were limited as to what I could do to support entrepreneurs, I would give them a way to kindle their vision, strengthen their tenacity, encourage their creativity, and motivate them to be courageous. In *Small Business Is Like A Bunch Of Bananas*, Jim Blasingame has done exactly that.

Jim has a unique way of speaking volumes in the 52 thoughts-in-a-nutshell in this book that takes the reader straight to the heart and spirit of entrepreneurialism. In this book, as in his radio/Internet broadcasts and other writings, Jim lifts up entrepreneurs and speaks to them on a level that can only be achieved by one who knows the world of small business.

If you own a small business, or are thinking about it, don't miss this opportunity to tap into Jim Blasingame's high entrepreneurial energy.

Good luck.

Steve Forbes
President and CEO, Forbes
Editor-in-Chief, FORBES Magazine

INTRODUCTION

I know what you're thinking: Why would anyone combine small business and bananas in the same sentence? Right? Well, truth is, not too many people would, but I'm afraid I have that kind of mind.

Of course, if you are already operating a small business, you might be thinking it makes perfect sense—the bananas, I mean—because you've seen things go bananas plenty of times in your business, especially when trying to make payroll on Friday. But that's not the kind of bananas I'm talking about.

I'm talking about bananas in terms of how we view the world, and how we approach the challenges we face in our small businesses. I'm not going to give it away here, because I want you to at least read the first chapter where I define the famous *Blasingame Banana Principle*. That's where you will see what I mean about bananas and small business.

Much has been said and written about how to run a small business. I know, because I am one of the people who has said and written much about those things. But this book is about you: the human behind the entrepreneurial dream; the one facing the challenges of operating a small business. The person with the bull's eye on top of the head where the proverbial "buck" keeps stopping.

And as much as anything else, this book is about your spirit.

You will find that word—spirit—recurring throughout everything I write or say about entrepreneurs. Here's why: When it seems that everything touching your entrepreneurial dream has gone south; when you have applied every business fundamental known to mankind and the challenge persists; that's when you will find out about your spirit.

The difference between entrepreneurs and everybody else is an ability and a desire to reach a little farther down inside themselves, to a place unfamiliar to mere mortals, where exists the capacity to persevere when marketplace pedestrians simply give up. The things I talk about in this book speak to that part of you.

I'm looking forward to having you become part of The Small Business Advocate community. I'll see you on the radio, or on the Internet.

Jim Blasingame
The Small Business Advocate

HOW TO USE THIS BOOK

Sometimes you need a motivational or inspirational lift and you don't want to read an entire book to get it. The ideas in this book have been written with that in mind. Easy to find. Short and sweet. Maximum message—minimum words. You're welcome.

To support this theme, the architecture of this book has each section beginning on the left-hand page so that, with only a handful of exceptions, you can read each one without turning a page.

Small Business Is Like A Bunch Of Bananas is composed of 52 thoughts, in case you want to focus on one per week. Or you can look in the Table of Contents for the issue that is on your mind.

If the ideas presented here should inspire a thought you want to remember, some of the pages have lines beside the words "Your Peels Here," where you can write them down. (Unless this is a library copy. You don't want to mess with a librarian.)

If a page you want to write on doesn't have lines, use the margins. This book is for you—use it!

Let the motivation and inspiration begin.

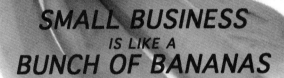

SMALL BUSINESS
IS LIKE A
BUNCH OF BANANAS
*You Have to Remove the Peels
to Get to the Good Stuff!*

SMALL BUSINESS IS LIKE
A BUNCH OF BANANAS

I like bananas any way you want to fix them: banana splits, banana sandwiches, bananas on my cereal, and of course, just a banana by itself. Once I even ate a banana dipped in chocolate. Mmm! Mmm!

But before I can eat a banana, I have some business to take care of—I have to lose the peel. A banana peel is actually a double problem: It tastes bad, and if you step on it, you will slip and fall. Everybody knows that. The banana peel has become our metaphor for danger underfoot.

So with two out of the three things I know about bananas being bad, when I see a banana why do I first think about how good it will taste? Why don't I dwell on the two negatives instead of the one positive? It's because I know that if I handle the banana correctly by removing the peel, including the strings (I hate those!), and properly dispose of it, I will have myself a pleasing and healthy result.

What if we looked at problems the way we look at bananas: A pleasing and healthy result wrapped in a distasteful and possibly dangerous peel? I've been in the marketplace long enough to feel qualified to say that many of the problems you and I will face in our small businesses won't have any worse odds than a banana—2:1, negative to positive. I call this the *Blasingame Banana Principle* (BBP).

So how do you apply the BBP? When you're presented with a problem, instead of dwelling on the consequences, imagine the possibilities. But just imagining won't get the job done. Just as with a banana, you must first deal with the possibility's peel.

Road test the BBP this week. Work on becoming an expert at properly disposing of your possibility's peel so you can get to the good stuff. If you can make the *Blasingame Banana Principle* your default approach to problems, I am convinced that your world will change.

> *Many of the problems you and I will face won't have any worse odds than a banana—2:1, negative to positive.*

By the way, I like my banana sandwiches plain, please; no mayonnaise or peanut butter.

THE LEADERSHIP COIN

Someone once told me that you can't be an effective leader without first knowing how to follow. I think successful leaders not only learn how to be followers first, but they also never forget that perspective.

In his book, *Moses: CEO*, my friend, Robert Dilenschneider, said:

Leading and following are opposite sides of the same coin.

What an interesting paradoxical metaphor: Opposites indeed, but one can't exist without the other. Being a leader takes more than just wanting to lead. In the marketplace, you can only be a leader if you can get others to follow you.

"A soldier will fight long and hard for a piece of colored ribbon."

- Napoleon

No matter the size of a small business, there will always be more things to do than people to do them—everyone must wear several different hats. You can't drive people to wear extra hats, but you can lead them to do it. Does this mean that leadership is an especially essential characteristic for a small business owner to have? I think so.

Napoleon once said, "A soldier will fight long and hard for a piece of colored ribbon." But only a leader who understands the heart of a follower can convince the soldier that the ribbon is worth fighting for.

If you want to be a successful small business owner, make sure you know and understand both sides of the leadership "coin." Then line up your troops, put your ribbon out in front, and lead them into battle.

Y
O
U
R

P
E
E
L
S

H
E
R
E

DON'T JUST MAKE CHANGES—EXPERIMENT

Remember when a calendar year could be used in the marketplace as the chronological parameter for a business cycle, or a marketing strategy? Remember when you could develop a product and count on the viability of the first generation lasting at least 12 months?

Well, that was a nice trip down memory lane, wasn't it?

Better buckle up. Today we measure business cycles in Internet terms, and an Internet year is about 90 days.

With so much market velocity, if our companies are going to survive, we have no choice but to change. But how does an organization accomplish so much change without killing everybody?

> *...how does an organization accomplish so much change without killing everybody?*

In *The Max Strategy*, Dale Dauten wrote:

> *... people hate to change, but they love to experiment.*

Eureka! That's the answer.

Don't just make changes—experiment with new paths to success. Change is annoying and tiresome. Experimenting is exciting because of the possibilities. You *give* your people change and *expect* them to accept it. But you *let* your people *participate* in an experiment.

Lose words like *change, different, new, improved,* and replace them with *experiment, create, participate, contribute.* This is not a word game—it's your new approach to making things happen without creating a casualty list.

As you contemplate your company's next new direction, project, or product, develop your approach around an *experiment.* And since you can't do it alone, be sure to use *all* of the brainpower and creative juices available from the people in your organization.

Change is what must happen. *Experimenting* is how you must do it.

ENJOY THE WHOLE TRIP

The richest person is the one who is contented with what he has.

- Robert C. Savage

I like that statement, but I can see how it would trouble those who are goal-oriented.

It's important to have goals. But if you are goal-oriented, that almost precludes being contented with what you have, doesn't it? So how do you reconcile Mr. Savage's sage observation with being goal-oriented? I think you do it by recognizing success in many different forms in your life.

Are you enjoying your current success, or has your impatience made you miss that once-in-a-lifetime opportunity?

You say, "I want to grow my company to $3 million in sales within three years." Good for you.

But while you're reaching for that next rung, are you recognizing that there are some pretty cool things to be appreciated about the rung you are on? Don't forget that just creating an organization that can realistically plan for such a goal is a pretty darn good success story.

Are you enjoying your current success, or has your impatience made you miss that once-in-a-lifetime opportunity? Don't be so anxious to reach the finish line. Remember, the operative word in that phrase is "finish."

Life is short. Enjoy the whole trip, including all of the stops.

Y
O
U
R

P
E
E
L
S

H
E
R
E

_____

_____

_____

_____

_____

BECOME THE SERVICE COIN OF THE REALM

In Jack Carew's book, *The Mentor*, I found this thought:

Become the "coin of the realm." Position yourself to be the obvious choice for doing business. Create such an outstanding customer-focused presence that people carry you around in their souls. This value-based relationship will provide you with a strong defense against your rivals.

The "coin of the realm" attitude should be more than just a personal goal; it should be instilled in your entire organization. If you deliver world-class service, when your customers need something you sell, the image in their minds will be of your company, or the face of someone in your organization, instead of the product or service.

With the "coin of the realm" philosophy of customer service in place, customer loyalty becomes your mint.

THE WORLD ACCORDING TO
JIM BLASINGAME

WRITE THIS ON A ROCK...

When opportunity knocks, it doesn't
know you've had a bad day.
Greet it with a smile.

BUMBLEBEES AND ENTREPRENEURS WANT TO FLY

I have always been an avid observer of wildlife. I like them all: mammals, reptiles, birds, fish, bugs, teenagers. Birds of prey are my favorite group, but I have to say that the critter I admire most is the lowly bumblebee, because bumblebees are not supposed to fly.

All of the experts, plus the rules of physics, aerodynamics, and gravity, point to the impossibility of this fat little guy leaving the ground with such inadequate wings. And yet, it flies.

Entrepreneurs are like bumblebees: Against all odds, and largely by their wits, entrepreneurs create successful businesses, often from absolutely nothing. All of the experts, plus the rules of business, finance, and the marketplace, point to the impossibility of such upstarts carving out a niche and flourishing. And yet, they flourish.

The experts and the rules have spoken: Bumblebees and entrepreneurs are not supposed to fly.

I don't know how many times I have heard a small business owner say, "When I started my business, I didn't know I wasn't supposed to be able to do this." That's why I like this quote from Bill O'Hanlon:

> *Most of the progress that's been made in human history has been by people who did not accept that something was impossible.*

The experts and the rules have spoken: It's impossible! Bumblebees and entrepreneurs are not supposed to fly.

WHAT'S THE MATTER WITH YOU TWO? CAN'T YOU READ???

Y
O
U
R

P
E
E
L
S

H
E
R
E

IDENTIFY YOUR BREAK POINT

In his book, *Rousing Creativity*, Floyd Hurt said:

> *It is not what we decide to do, but how we decide it that matters.*

Floyd calls this concept a "break point" because, "...it demands a break in the motion of your thinking and actions." He further says, "...it also means a break from the way you have done things in the past."

Let's say you have a decision to make. You've gathered the facts and it's time to decide. But when the facts are altered by how you see them—good or bad—Floyd calls that "baggage."

Make sure the decisions you make are grounded in your research, but focused on the future.

The marketplace is moving *very* fast. Make sure the decisions you make are grounded in your research, but focused on the future. Not so much about the world you know, as much as the world you are entering. The *what* part of your decision is empirical, but the *how* must be about your ability to shed your baggage and focus on the future.

Good decisions result when you can learn how to separate these two—at the break point.

Y
O
U
R

P
E
E
L
S

H
E
R
E

_____

_____

_____

_____

_____

_____

_____

CONSCIOUS OR UNCONSCIOUS?

Learning about the four levels of competence many years ago was a real watershed experience for me.

They are:

- Unconscious Incompetent
- Conscious Incompetent
- Unconscious Competent
- Conscious Competent

The first and last levels are the most important.

An Unconscious Incompetent is a person who doesn't know that he doesn't know—a k a "don't know[2]."

...being a Conscious Competent takes a desire to learn and to grow, and a passion to achieve excellence.

Before you get too smug—sure that I couldn't be talking about you—if you are learning every day, you are capable of being a "don't know[2]" every day.

So the objective is not so much to *never* be an Unconscious Incompetent—reaching out to new possibilities can put you, at least temporarily, in that condition. But rather you should try to be *conscious* of what you know and don't know, so that you don't live your life in a state of Unconscious Incompetence.

Confucius said:

To know what you know, and know what you don't know, is the characteristic of one who knows.

Two and a half millennia ago, the great sage was defining and teaching the importance of being a Conscious Competent.

But being a Conscious Competent takes more than just being conscious. It takes a desire to learn and to grow, and a passion to achieve excellence.

ADAPT OR BECOME EXTINCT

Have you ever said, "I don't know what I want to be when I grow up"? Of course, we all have. Have you ever thought of those words as limiting? Taken literally, they indicate that you will only be one thing when you grow up.

Don't misunderstand: Having a goal is both admirable and eminently practical. No one should be sailing around, willy-nilly, without a professional or personal rudder.

In today's marketplace, however, most of us will not only change jobs several times in a career, we will likely change industries more than once. Consequently, it can be professionally dangerous to limit our energy and resources to a narrow field of endeavor.

Darwin's theory of natural selection is alive and well in the marketplace, and in society.

Too narrow a focus can also be boring. A life lived should be much more than what you want to be when you grow up. Theologian, philosopher, and author, Alan Watts, once said:

> *Thinking that the self must remain constant for life to have meaning is like falling help-lessly in love with an inch.*

Unless you're an inchworm, I hope this doesn't sound like you. I believe in the importance of, and potential for, personal evolution. I intend to be a different person today than I was ten years ago, and look forward to the changes of the next ten.

Darwin's theory of natural selection is alive and well in the marketplace and in society: Adapt or become extinct—grow or become boring. If you become the latter, your subsequent extinction will go unnoticed.

Y
O
U
R

P
E
E
L
S

H
E
R
E

VICTORY OVER DOUBT

You are my enemy, Doubt!

You are my anti-energy,
my nemesis,
and the lie that lays me low.

You dwell in the valleys between my aspirations,
you steal from my spirit,
and taunt me from the shadows with your cache of lies.

You are insidious, Doubt!

The pain of your itch is sweetly seductive,
and you lure me in with
painful pleasure when I scratch you.

The weight of your influence is burdensome,
the sense of your negativism is frightening,
and the pull of your gravity is maddening.

You will be silent, Doubt!

You invade my dreams,
you linger in my consciousness,
and you attack my hopes.

You have no important message,
redeeming value,
or concern for my well-being.

You will not succeed, Doubt!

You will fail to control me;
you will scarce be more than a word that I know,
rather than a force that defines me.

If I am to be myself
you cannot own me,
or hold me hostage.

You will not win, Doubt!

I will refuse your discouragement,
and deny you access to
the possibilities that lie ahead for me.

Above your protests, I will focus on my capabilities,
recognize my accomplishments,
and rise to face challenges and opportunities.

You are in my way, Doubt!

I have things to create,
ideas to deliver,
and destiny to fulfill.

The ship of my vision is rigged,
a tide of momentum is rising,
and you are excess ballast.

You will not defeat me, Doubt!

I will remember the words of Kahlil Gibran,
"Doubt is a pain too lonely to know
that faith is his twin brother."

I will fight you with my faith,
obscure you with my creativity,
and defeat you with my spirit and with my will.

Get behind me, Doubt!

I am greater than you, Doubt!

I believe in myself!

THE WORLD ACCORDING TO
JIM BLASINGAME

WRITE THIS ON A ROCK...

*In the marketplace, you can only
be a leader if you can get
others to follow you.*

THE RIGHT STUFF

I expect to maintain this contest until success-
ful, or till I die, or am conquered, or my term
expires, or Congress or the country forsakes me.
                                    - Abraham Lincoln

Sound familiar? If you are a small business owner, I'll bet it sounds very familiar. It might even give you a little chill when you read these 140-year-old words—hearing the essence of your being translated into the spoken word in a way in which you may never have actually spoken it out loud.

When I was an officer in the U.S. Army, I was trained to be responsible for "everything my unit does, or fails to do." It's the same for small business owners—you turn the lights on, you turn the lights off. Tenaciously doing whatever it takes.

The tenacious have the courage of their convictions.

Tenacity. I sure do like that word. And I admire tenacious people—they have the courage of their convictions. Courage, passion, and a strong, indomitable spirit. Are you tenacious?

If you are a small business owner, you know how far down inside you that you have to reach to rise above all of the challenges, train wrecks, and surprises that are thrown at you. Sometimes deeper than you knew you could. Testing your mettle.

I don't care what anybody says—astronauts are heroes, but they don't own the franchise on "the right stuff." Small business owners have it, too.

I am so proud of you.

Y
O
U
R

P
E
E
L
S

H
E
R
E

RISK WHAT YOU KNOW

Ever wonder what makes someone ... take risks? ... take the next step? ... have a go at something they've never tried before? I ask myself these questions, mostly about myself, all the time.

This jewel is from my friend, Tom Feltenstein, and it's in his book, *Uncommon Wisdom*:

> *The times when I've been truly creative—when I've been the boldest and most imaginative, when I've taken the lead—have been those times when I was willing not to know. When I was willing to risk what I knew, for what I might learn.*

I believe the ability to "risk what I know, for what I might learn" is the essence of entrepreneurialism. And in the not knowing, but going forward anyway, we find the conjoined, twin emotions of fear and exhilaration.

The Twins presage possibility: Might be good—might not be. Might be extremely successful—might be a train wreck. And contemplating the possibility produces the head-rush entrepreneurs get at the moment they risk what they know for what they might learn.

You will never hear me minimize doing research. An entrepreneur's hunch without some foundation of research is like a belt without belt loops. Some entrepreneurs take risks; smart entrepreneurs take calculated risks. Still, there comes a time, especially for entrepreneurs, when you must take action even though you don't have all the answers.

...in the not knowing, but going forward anyway, you find the conjoined, twin emotions of fear and exhilaration.

The difference in entrepreneurs, therefore, is in how long each one can wait for answers before taking action: How the point of possibility is defined, and when to risk what is known for what might be learned.

To know, or to act? That is the question.

SLOW DOWN—LISTEN TO YOUR WISDOM

I found this thought in Joseph Bailey's book, *The Speed Trap*:

> *You don't have to be a genius to have wisdom; it is available to all of us. When your mind spins out of control, let go and trust that the wisdom within you will guide you back to happiness. Wisdom is true genius.*

One of the benefits of getting older is that, presumably, we also get wiser. Humans of all ages react to most things from either of three locations in their being: head, heart, and gut—or instinct. I believe wisdom might simply be knowing which one to listen to.

Head, heart, and gut—or instinct...wisdom might simply be knowing which one to listen to.

For small business owners, it's not always easy to employ our wisdom. We are often pulled in several directions at once, while simultaneously feeling crushed by the stress and pressures that come with this life we have chosen and cherish. The challenge is to find the discipline to let our wisdom work.

When things are the most hectic, try to slow down. Give the wisdom you have acquired time to work. Wisdom is best employed after a deep breath, at a minimum, and a night's sleep, at the optimum.

If you learn how to use your wisdom, you can be a genius. Joe Bailey said so.

Y
O
U
R

P
E
E
L
S

H
E
R
E

_____

_____

_____

_____

_____

_____

FOCUS ON YOUR GAUGES

In his book, *This Is Your Life, Not A Dress Rehearsal*, Jim Donovan said:

> *One of the chief characteristics of virtually all highly successful people is that they make decisions quickly, and rarely, if ever, change them.*

This might seem like a rigid, perhaps even arrogant attitude—to refuse to change a decision—but there is something else at work here.

One of the keys to success is to be able to make things happen. In order to do this, you have to make a lot of decisions. If you know what you are doing, you will make most of them correctly. Incorrect decisions aren't so much failures, as they are examples of what doesn't work.

Successful people make lots of decisions, and trust that they will either lead to success, or the next decision.

When you learn to fly an airplane on instruments (when you are in the "soup" and you can't see outside of the plane), as you monitor your gauges and controls, you are taught to make little corrections when you see the plane drifting off course or out of your assigned altitude. You must make lots of little corrections, and you must make them constantly.

My instrument instructor told me, "Focus on your gauges, trust them, and make little corrections—constantly." The result is that your plane never gets too far off course, or into an unsafe attitude.

Successful people do the same thing in their businesses. They make lots of decisions. And while it may seem that they rarely change a decision, it's really more a matter of moving on and making the next decision with new information. Little corrections, but lots of them. Constantly.

Sometimes it feels as if we are managing our businesses in the soup. And just like a pilot on instruments, it's natural to freeze up at first. When you get this feeling, focus on your gauges—the decisions that have to be made. Then make lots of decisions, and trust them to either lead you to success or the next decision.

Good flying.

SPIRIT AND HEART

If you are going to be a successful small business owner, you need the spirit of an entrepreneur *and* the heart of an operator.

An entrepreneurial spirit helps you imagine and then create your business. But it takes the heart of an operator to stick with your business when you have to attend to the everyday, mundane things like accounting, banking, credit policies, personnel issues, prospecting, etc.

Spirit *and* heart—you will need both.

Y
O
U
R

P
E
E
L
S

H
E
R
E

THE WORLD ACCORDING TO
JIM BLASINGAME

WRITE THIS ON A ROCK...

Darwin's theory of natural selection
is alive and well in the marketplace:
Adapt or become extinct.

KNOWLEDGE WILL MAKE YOU SMILE

Training is everything. The peach was once a bitter almond, and cauliflower is nothing but a cabbage with a college education.

- Mark Twain

After all these years there has been no one to compare with Twain, and the light of his wisdom has not dimmed.

No matter what we do or where we go, owner or employee, and now more than ever before, we must continue to study, train, and learn. Everyone in your organization. *Everyone.* Everyday. Lifelong learning.

When I feel threatened by all of the new information and capability that's emerging, I just make a point to learn something new...

Are you feeling threatened these days—maybe even frightened—because of all the changes brought on by the advent of the information age? Me, too. Sometimes it seems we're like Alice—we have to run as fast as we can just to stay in one place. And in *our* Wonderland, everything is changing so fast that what we learn today may be obsolete tomorrow.

The irony is that the thing that is creating so much potential for anxiety—technology—is also the thing that can help you stay competitive. And the unprecedented wealth of information available on the Internet is a two edged sword: one side cutting for us, and the other for our competition.

When I feel threatened by all of the new information and capability that's emerging, I just make a point to learn something new, with emphasis on e-commerce, or the Internet, or how my industry is adapting to the virtual marketplace. And when I acquire that new understanding or capability, I smile like Alice's Cheshire Cat.

Learning makes me feel stronger, as if I've gained a little ground in the marketplace. Maybe today I'll put the heat on somebody else. Advantage: Me.

Give it a try. The only thing better than your garden variety smile is one that comes from knowing that you just got a little smarter.

I have to say, however, cauliflower does not make me smile.

LOOKING UP FROM THE MUD

In 1066 AD, the Duke of Normandy, William I (the Conqueror) was about to lay claim to England on the field of battle against King Harold. As he led his men ashore in southeast England, toward what was to become the Battle of Hastings, the would-be king, rather ignominiously, stumbled and fell face-first into the mud.

Looking up from the mud, seeing "Bad Omen" written all over the faces of his superstitious men, the future king of England stood up, displayed his muddied hands, and cried, "By the splendor of God, I have taken possession of my realm; the earth of England is in my two hands."

Our character is not measured by falls, but rather by how we handle ourselves after the fall, with mud on our hands.

As business owners, we often stumble. A fall for us is a mistake or an unfortunate circumstance, and both are abiding elements in the marketplace, as well as in life.

In truth, the question is not whether we will stumble, fall, and muddy our hands, because all three are virtually ordained. Our character is not measured by falls, but rather by how we handle ourselves after the fall, with mud on our hands.

Some things haven't changed much in a thousand years. There are still plenty of people around watching to see how a leader reacts after a misstep.

When you look up from the mud, do you complain, make excuses, blame others, (your whine here)? Or do you behave as William the Conqueror did: Stand up, assess the damage, accept the circumstances, remember that you are a leader on whom others depend, and drive on to win the day?

One more thing: It also doesn't hurt if, like William, you can think fast.

Y
O
U   _____
R

P   _____
E
E
L   _____
S

H   _____
E
R
E   _____

GO AHEAD—LAUGH AT YOURSELF

It is of immense importance to laugh at ourselves.
                                        - Katherine Mansfield

I fully subscribe to this philosophy. Indeed, if I didn't laugh at myself I would miss the best laughs of my life.

Can you do it—laugh at yourself? It doesn't come easily for some. You might have to practice, but there are definite benefits.

Laughing at yourself humanizes you to those who live, work, and associate with you, and it disarms your detractors. And, in those rare moments when you are less than perfect, laughing at yourself can actually cut you some slack, and turn a pregnant moment or a *faux pas* into an opportunity to bond. Sounds like a pretty handy tool to me. What do you think?

> *Laughing at yourself humanizes you to those who live, work, and associate with you, and it disarms your detractors.*

We all do things that are unintended. When that happens, so will laughter—whether right in front of you, or later behind your back. Either way, it will be at your expense, so you might as well participate.

Don't take yourself too seriously. That next mistake you are already dreading could become the best laugh you've had all day.

Y
O
U
R

P
E
E
L
S

H
E
R
E

SPROUT AN IDEA SEED

A seed is such an interesting thing. It emerges as a soft, fleshy issue from the parent, then morphs into a dry, hardened kernel in order to withstand time and travel until the day when its purpose in life, germination, begins.

Think of it: A tiny kernel of wheat can become the staff of life. An acorn, no larger than your thumbnail, holds the genetic code and capacity to grow into the towering organism which has become our metaphor for strength—the mighty oak tree.

When you imagine something, you sprout an idea seed. When you dream of an accomplishment, you become the parent of an idea seed.

An idea seed begins as a soft and fleshy musing, then germinates into what might nourish your next great idea.

An idea seed begins as a soft and fleshy musing, then with time and travel, hardens into the kernel of a concept that is ready to germinate into what might become your next great idea. Or it may hold all of the inspirational code necessary to become the mighty oak-of-an-idea upon which you will build your life, your business, your future.

In his book, *The Seven Spiritual Laws of Success*, Deepak Chopra said:

> *Within every desire is the seed and mechanics for its fulfillment.*

You not only have the ability to sprout an idea seed, but with desire and focus, you have the mechanism to germinate it into something useful.

Thinking of ideas as seeds helps me collect them, categorize them, and use them at the right time and for the right purpose. Like seeds, ideas aren't always ready to open up at first. And some ideas, like seeds, shouldn't be used for awhile.

As you begin collecting idea seeds, create the kind of mental, fertile soil that will allow them to germinate at the right time and for the right purpose, each in its own time.

ON TOP OF A FENCE POST

Awhile back I heard someone accept an award by telling this story:

> *I once saw a turtle on top of a fence post. The first thing that struck me was that the turtle surely had not gotten there by himself.*

The gentleman went on to accept the award on behalf of all those who had helped him get to the top of his "fence post."

If you are the owner, employer, and/or manager of a team of people, next time you find yourself on top of a fence post, make sure that you recognize the others who helped you to reach your lofty perch.

Not only is it the right thing to do, but remember, Newton's law of gravity is especially active around fence posts.

It's handy to have people around who will want to break your fall in case you find yourself experiencing Mr. Newton's law in an untimely descent from on high.

THE WORLD ACCORDING TO
JIM BLASINGAME

WRITE THIS ON A ROCK...

Whether your mistakes are valuable
or expensive depends on whether
you contemplate and learn from
them, or deny and keep
on paying for them.

USE YOUR UNIQUENESS

Do you spend a lot of time worrying about what others think of your ideas? If you have what you think is a great idea, something you are passionate about, do you drop it when someone else shoots it down?

Obviously, it's good to bounce ideas off of those you trust. But ultimately, you are the best judge of your own idea.

Did you know that Dr. Seuss's first children's book was rejected 23 times? If he hadn't believed in his idea, the world might never have known about Sam and his green eggs and ham.

In his book, *The Mentor*, Jack Carew wrote:

> *Use your uniqueness. What you do and how you do it is distinct and special.*

Listen and learn, but don't discount "your uniqueness."

Try as they might, others may not be able to properly evaluate your unique way of looking at something. More than likely, they will focus on the *thing* and not the unique way you see it.

Of course, do your research. Of course, talk with other

people. But not so much to find out if what you are thinking is a good idea, as much as to find out how to make improvements. Listen and learn, but don't discount your uniqueness.

Now—I've got this idea to sell green milk. Whaddaya think?

Y
O
U
R

P
E
E
L
S

H
E
R
E

FOCUS FORWARD

In the world of runners, there are two kinds: sprinters and distance runners. To be sure, sprinters must train long and hard to be successful. But when it comes to the actual event, in 10 to 40 seconds it's over. Raw, explosive muscle power pushing the body to the extreme, but not much mental taxation.

Like sprinters, distance runners have to train plenty. But their event often seems as much a test of mind, spirit, and will as it is a demonstration of conditioning, strength, and endurance.

Small business owners are more like distance runners than sprinters. Even if we have the fundamentals (strength) and the experience (conditioning), all of the stuff that we have to deal with, sometimes all alone, sorely tests our spiritual mettle (endurance). Like a distance runner, a small business owner often moves forward more on sheer will than anything else.

> *If you can't solve next week's problems today, don't let them trip you up today.*

In his book, *What's The Rush?*, James Ballard wrote this thought about focus:

When you feel overwhelmed and want to quit,
pick out a landmark just ahead—a light pole,
a house, a tree—and agree to run only that far.

Jim is a runner, but his words are meant for every test of our strength and will. I use this mental drill when it looks like I am more likely to be prey than predator. I make an agreement with myself to just take things one day at a time— sometimes one hour at a time—and it helps me stay focused on the present stretch of the race.

However far ahead you place your "light pole," focusing on that way-point instead of the finish line will help your mettle withstand the stress.

You can't cross the finish line halfway through the race. If you can't solve next week's problems today, don't let them trip you up today.

I have a little prayer that helps me get to my next light pole: "You and me, Lord, one day at a time."

On your mark—get set—go!

YOUR PERSONAL HORIZON

A horizon is such a useful thing—it helps you have perspective in your life.

There is more than one kind, you know: The old standby that meets the sky as you drive down the road or sail on the water, for one. In aviation, there is an artificial horizon—a gauge that pilots use to keep their aircraft in the desired attitude when they are in the "soup" and can't see horizon #1.

Then there is what I call your *Personal Horizon*, PH for short. Your PH is your perspective on future prospects—where you are headed in your personal and professional life.

You don't have to go anywhere to change your Personal Horizon. You can do it right now, right where you are.

Do you see a bright horizon, with clearly defined features, or do you see a dark and hazy horizon, where you are not sure of what's ahead?

When you are on the ground, if you want a better view you have to physically move to higher ground in the hopes of gaining a better perspective. You can improve your PH by moving to higher ground in your life through education, new goals, a new attitude, etc.

In his book, *As You Think*, James Allen wrote:

You will become as great as your dominant aspiration. If you cherish a vision, a lofty ideal in your heart, you will realize it.

I'm not saying that changing yourself is easy, but you have to admit, it is convenient. You don't have to physically go anywhere to change your PH. You can do it right now, right where you are.

Allow your aspirations to become dominant. Give your vision a chance to work by acquiring a new PH.

Where do you look for your Personal Horizon? James Allen says it's "in your heart."

"DEAR" MISTAKES

*Those things are dearest to us that have cost
us the most.*

- Michel de Montaigne

Could the great Renaissance thinker have been talking about mistakes? I think so. Do you think of your mistakes as "dear"?

Mistakes are worth contemplating, and yet we often don't. The reason, I think, is because it hurts a little to focus on them. It's not fun to see ourselves that way. Mistakes are definitely not ego food.

But there is something very important to remember about mistakes: not focusing on them can ultimately be more painful.

If you don't contemplate your mistakes and learn from them, you are subjecting yourself to double jeopardy.

If you don't contemplate your mistakes and learn from them, you are subjecting yourself to double jeopardy. Because today you will not only make the new mistakes you are destined to make as you go through life, but you are also doomed to repeat the old ones you should have learned from yesterday.

Whether your mistakes are valuable or expensive depends on whether you contemplate and learn from them, or deny and keep on paying for them.

I think paying for a mistake once is "dear" enough, don't you?

Y
O
U
R

P
E
E
L
S

H
E
R
E

EINSTEIN AND SMALL BUSINESS

Small is the number of them who see with their own eyes and feel with their own hearts. But it is their strength that will decide whether the human race must relapse into the state of stupor which a deluded multitude appears today to regard as the ideal.

- Albert Einstein

I believe small business owners are well represented in Mr. Einstein's small number. Every day you forge your vision and passion into an entrepreneurial alloy that is strong and productive.

Don't ever forget this, small business owners: Through your eyes, opportunity is born. From your heart, "the ideal" is defined and attained.

You make a difference—one person, one job, one customer at a time.

I think Mr. Einstein would have been proud of you. He was a genius, you know.

THE WORLD ACCORDING TO
JIM BLASINGAME

WRITE THIS ON A ROCK...

Are you enjoying your current success, or has your impatience for the next goal made you miss that once-in-a-lifetime opportunity?

HOW IS YOUR TRACTOR BUSINESS?

The great 20th-century entrepreneur, Henry Ford, made a trip to Europe during World War I to try to encourage the combatants to end the war. Before long he was back in the U.S., rather frustrated and disappointed in the result of his mission. But he later made the following observation:

> *I didn't get much peace, but I found out that Russia is going to be a great market for tractors.*

By this time in his life, Mr. Ford probably wasn't surprised when the pursuit of one project (which failed) produced information, if not opportunity, for another.

You must make yourself available to the possibilities.

It's impossible to know where or when your next revelation, discovery, or new opportunity is going to occur. The next phone call could provide valuable information for your business. The next person you meet could become the newest member of your company's brain trust. The next words you hear or read could trigger some clearer view into a previously murky perspective. The next annoying problem you face could turn into a life changing opportunity.

I think Mr. Ford would tell you that none of this happens if you don't engage the world. You must make yourself available to the possibilities.

Remember, when opportunity knocks, it's often disguised as something else. And if you're not there when it comes calling, opportunity doesn't leave a message. It moves on.

How's *your* tractor business these days?

Y
O
U
R

P
E
E
L
S

H
E
R
E

TIP YOUR MENTAL "IN" BASKET

Harold Alexander, British field marshal during WWII and First Earl of Tunis, had a habit at the end of the day of "tipping" the remaining work left in his IN basket into his OUT basket. When asked why he did this he replied, "It saves time, and you'd be surprised at how much doesn't come back."

As small business owners, the Earl's management style could be dangerous. Besides, many of us don't have anyone to come by and get the stuff out of our OUT basket. If we don't do it, it doesn't get done.

...at the end of each day, tip all of your leftover problems into your mind's OUT basket.

But I wonder about this method for dealing with worry.

What if, at the end of each day, you tipped all of your leftover problems into your mind's OUT basket: the problem customers, the bank payment, the new competitor. Go ahead, put all of those alligators right in there. Don't worry. The ones that need to be will be there in the morning. But you might be surprised at the ones that just don't come back. And there you were worrying about them. Pretty silly, huh?

In his book, *Blue Highways*, William Least Heat-Moon Trogden reported that his grandfather, who was full-blooded American Indian (Osage), once told him:

> *Some things don't have to be remembered,*
> *they remember themselves.*

So, there you have it. If it's important, it will be there in the morning. If not, it will go away and wasn't worth the worry.

Worry is one of the greatest inner demons small business owners have to slay. Give that "tipping" thing a try. It just might save you some worry.

Now where did I put that OUT basket?

HAPPINESS[2]

Did you know that there is actually a level of happiness—higher than your garden variety happiness—that can be attained by knowing that you are happy and knowing why you are happy? Henry Miller wrote in *Colossus of Maroussi:*

> *It is good to be happy; it's a little better to know that you're happy; but to understand that you're happy and know why and how ... and still be happy, be happy in the being and the knowing, well that is beyond happiness, that is bliss.*

I like this thought, but reading it made me coin a new term: Happiness[2] (or H^2)—being happy and knowing why you are happy. I like that better than bliss. Bliss is such a presumptuous word, don't you think?

...think about what is most important in your life; because that is where your happiness comes from.

Here's the question: What makes you happy? No, really—think about it this time. Close your eyes, take two deep breaths, and think about what is most important in your life, because that is where your happiness comes from. Might be children, work, creating, your faith, things like that. Not money. Not stuff. If money and stuff are what you think makes you happy, I propose that you aren't really happy.

Here's the challenge: Work hard, create, build, and yes, make money, too. But don't forget where real happiness comes from. Work on attaining some of that H^2.

Y
O
U
R

P
E
E
L
S

H
E
R
E

_____

_____

_____

_____

_____

_____

MAKE A DIFFERENCE TO JUST ONE

Even in America, the land of plenty, there are so many people who need food, shelter, a helping hand, and a kind word. It's true that the safety net created by public and private organizations is multilayered and highly efficient, but it is just a net after all, not a pillow. Nets have holes.

Looking at the many un-met needs, it's easy to be intimidated by the scale, and we feel justified in our indifference because, "Hey, I pay my taxes and contribute to charities, don't I? What more can I do? I'm just one person."

...at least once a day, try to make a difference in another person's life.

I like this story, paraphrased from *The Star Thrower* by Loren Eiseley. See what you think.

A man was walking on a familiar stretch of beach one morning after a storm, and up ahead he could see a stranger coming toward him. The stranger was continually stooping over, picking up something, and tossing it in the ocean. Finally, the man could see that the stranger was throwing some of the thousands of tiny starfish the storm had washed up on the beach.

As the two men drew near and exchanged greetings,

the man commended the stranger for his efforts, but also commented on the futility of such a task. "There must be hundreds of thousands of starfish on this beach. How could one person possibly make a difference?"

Picking up another tiny starfish and tossing it back into the ocean, the stranger answered, "Made a difference to that one, didn't I?"

Here's a pledge I will make to you and ask you to consider making:

> *As I race through my hectic life, at least once a day I will try to make a difference in another person's life.*

Could be as simple as holding a door, patting a back, giving a compliment, noticing a frown. Or perhaps something a little more involved like checking on someone with a call or visit, creating an opportunity, providing a meal, (your starfish here).

With a world so full of un-met needs, at the end of the day at least we would be able to say, "Made a difference to that one, didn't I?"

SMALL BUSINESS DREAMS

The British playwright, William Archer (1856-1924), once remarked to a friend about how a perfect plot had played out to him and evolved in a dream one night. He saw the whole thing, from beginning to end, and when he awoke, put pen to paper.

Small business owners know about this kind of dream. It begins with what I call the "founding dream," which is the first time a subconscious entrepreneurial inclination pops up on the consciousness radar screen.

At first, a founding dream may be barely discernible. And when it is remembered, the awareness is often more troubling than remarkable: "What does this mean? What do I do with it?"

But if the mind and the spirit are receptive, a founding dream evolves into more than a blip on the radar. Subsequent dreams become less impressionistic and more representative.

Animated dreams come next. Your nocturnal entrepreneurial visions play out with an actual cast of characters— sometimes in Technicolor™. Now you are well aware of, and more comfortable with, your small business dreams, and you start to do a little daydreaming.

Daydreaming is the first step in the due diligence process—the research. You start asking lots of questions: "What if ... ?" "How do I ... ?" "Who can ... ?" "When should ... ?" "Where does this ... ?"

Ultimately, armed with answers to these questions, you make your entrepreneurial dreams become reality: You begin living the dream of owning your own business.

At this point you might think you would stop dreaming—since you are living your dream, why dream about it? But make no mistake, the dreams are there! Now they just manifest themselves differently, in at least two ways:

> *Subconscious dreams are for things of whimsy. Your dream has come true, and there's nothing whimsical about it.*

1. The passion in your entrepreneurial dreams will be so strong they actually wake you up—at 2 or 3 a.m.
2. And whether at 3 a.m. or when the alarm goes off, you wake up with an idea, a question, or an answer.

Subconscious dreams are for things of whimsy. *Your* dream has come true, and there's nothing whimsical about it. Your dream now has a name, address, phone number, and a tax ID number.

As your entrepreneurial dream plays out in front of you, be sure to let your conscious actions consider what your subconscious tells you. Blend the facts your research produces with the ideas, questions, and answers that you woke up with this morning. Then, like the playwright, create the perfect plot for your small business.

Y
O
U
R

P
E
E
L
S

H
E
R
E

_____

_____

_____

_____

_____

_____

_____

THE WORLD ACCORDING TO
JIM BLASINGAME

WRITE THIS ON A ROCK...

*An idea seed may hold all of the
inspirational code necessary to
become the mighty oak-of-an-idea
upon which you will build your life,
your business, your future.*

SMALL BUSINESS'S INVISIBLE HAND

The most celebrated passage in Adam Smith's 1776 classic, *The Wealth of Nations*, is about something Smith called "the invisible hand." The invisible hand is the inadvertent but ultimate benevolence that communities and countries enjoy as a result of the economic self-interest of individuals and companies conducting business in the marketplace.

Smith wrote:

> *... led by an invisible hand ..., an individual pursuing his own interest in the marketplace, ... frequently promotes that of the society more effectually than when he really intends to promote it.*

Smith didn't mean that individuals are indifferent to all the good things the invisible hand leads them and their businesses to do for society. He was merely, but brilliantly, identifying one of the subtle, but powerful dividends that accrue to societies from free markets.

Imagine the impact of small business's invisible hand on America: Comprising over 98% of all U.S. businesses

(SBA), you employ over 60% of all employees (NFIB), and produce over 50% of the Gross National Product (SBA). Small businesses are millions of very visible hands creating most of the leverage for the invisible hand to work its benevolence in our society.

> Imagine the impact of small business's invisible hand...

Small business owners, you've created a lot of visible things to be proud of. In addition to the production of goods and services, you've created jobs, wealth, quality of life, etc. Now you know that you have at least one *invisible* thing to be proud of.

Y
O
U
R

_____

P
E
E
L
S

_____

_____

H
E
R
E

_____

_____

WILL AND FAITH

I like this anonymous thought:

The only thing that stands between a man and what he wants from life is often merely the will to try it, and the faith to believe that it is possible.

Will and faith. Two powerful little words that, unfortunately, are not often used in the marketplace these days.

Human will is an anthropological alloy forged of spirit, desire, and conscience. It is an invisible force deep inside you that makes things happen in your life. Faith, it has been said, is believing in something you can't see. Faith in yourself is faith in your will.

> **Human will is an anthropological alloy forged of spirit, desire, and conscience.**

But if will is the atomic power of your existence, without faith, it is inert.

If you want to see a demonstration of will and faith working together, go watch small business owners. Here's what you will see: A will that drives them to create things and accomplish feats lesser mortals are barely able to dream about, in tandem with a faith that allows them to keep going when most others would accept defeat.

Small business owners, like bumblebees, don't know that they aren't supposed to fly. And yet they do. Powered by will, on the aerodynamics of faith, small business owners fly their dreams every day.

It's a beautiful thing.

Y
O
U
R

P
E
E
L
S

H
E
R
E

WORK = LIFE

Have you ever thought about why we work? Obviously, food, shelter, and other necessities are one answer. But beyond that, why do we work?

The title of my favorite chapter in Jim McCann's book, *Stop And Sell The Roses,* is, "Work = Life." How do you feel about that philosophy?

To help put this idea in perspective, let's substitute *work* with some sexier words:

Money and stuff are just ways to keep score.

Money = Life
Boat = Life
House = Life
Jewelry = Life
Car = Life
Cruise = Life

As nice as these things may be, as a philosophy of life, they just don't have that "reason for being" impact, do they?

Now try these:

Productivity = Life
Innovation = Life
Service = Life

Challenge = Life
Creativity = Life
Contribution = Life

Much better, don't you think? These words create a more appealing perspective on why we go to work every day, don't they?

Money and stuff are just ways to keep score.

Work = Life.

Y
O
U
R

P
E
E
L
S

H
E
R
E

_____

_____

_____

_____

_____

_____

PASSION AND PANIC

You're living your entrepreneurial dream, following your vision, and road testing your plan. You have carved something out of the marketplace that wasn't there before. Congratulations.

But...you haven't yet reached the point where you *know* that all of your effort and sacrifice will have been worth it. Your business is young and, truth is, the jury is still out on whether you will survive.

The most anguishing emotion in the market-place is the one felt by entrepreneurs when they are faced with the possibility of failure.

You are in the bipolar stage of small business: One minute you're awash in passion, intensity, and the conviction that what you are doing is near genius, and the next minute you're telling yourself that you must be out of your mind to take such risks. The two faces of entrepreneurialism: passion and panic.

The most anguishing emotion in the marketplace is the one felt by entrepreneurs when they are faced with the possibility of failure. "How far do I go? How far CAN I go? How will I know if I have to...NO! I refuse to think about that!"

Here are some words of resolve from an anonymous thinker that I want to leave you with:

> *The wayside of business is littered with the remains of those who started with a spurt, but lacked the stamina to finish. Their places were taken by those unshowy plodders who never know when to quit.*

Which one are you?

Welcome to the world of small business ownership. One thing we never have to worry about is nodding off in the middle of the day.

FAILURE—AN ABIDING PART OF LIFE

In *Uncommon Wisdom*, my friend, Tom Feltenstein wrote:

> *When winners fail, they get up and go again.*
> *And the very act of getting up is victory.*

Developing that thought, Tom quotes Robert Allen:

> *There is no failure, only feedback.*

And then completes his thought with this:

> *Failure is successfully discovering something*
> *that doesn't work.*

Words of wisdom that can only come from those who have known failure, and from that acquaintance, found success.

I like to think of failure as the harness-mate of success, and I expect to be hitched to both as long as I live.

THE WORLD ACCORDING TO
JIM BLASINGAME

WRITE THIS ON A ROCK...

Many of the problems you and I face won't have any worse odds than a banana—2:1, negative to positive. But you have to remove the peel to get to the good stuff.
- The Blasingame Banana Principle

LEAN LIBERTY—FAT SLAVERY

An ancient proverb proposes that...

Lean liberty is better than fat slavery.

Many small business owners would say it this way, "The worst day in my own business is better than the best day as an employee."

Even though I'm not proposing that employment is akin to slavery, there is no question it can put chains on your entrepreneurial spirit. But before you become a runaway from your job because you don't like bosses, or decide to emancipate your creativity from mediocre management, let's refer to Blasingame's Small Business Unabridged Dictionary, and portions of its definition of "lean liberty" in the world of small business:

> *When an employee doesn't show up for a shift, it's your shift.*

1. "The Buck Stops Here" plaque is not just sitting on your desk, it's nailed down.
2. When an employee doesn't show up for a shift, it's *your* shift.

3. When an irate, perhaps unreasonable, customer comes in and demands to speak to the owner...that's you.

4. It's payroll Friday for you and your three employees. Four people, but only enough cash for three checks. Guess who goes home without one?

If any part of this definition makes you blink, be sure to clock in tomorrow.

But if you are ready to handle these and many other examples of small business "lean liberty," perhaps your entrepreneurial sap has risen to the point where your passion for your business will sustain you through the lean times. Go for it.

Who knows? You may be on your way to claim the Holy Grail of small business, "Fat Liberty."

PUSHING THE ENVELOPE

*A mind stretched by a new idea never returns
to its original dimension.*

- James Lincoln

This quote reminds me of an aviation term, "pushing the envelope."

Flying an aircraft within its predetermined performance parameters keeps you inside the operating envelope, and presumably safe. Operating outside these parameters is called "pushing the envelope," and it is usually only done intentionally by test pilots, to establish the envelope.

In life, are you a test pilot who pushes the envelope, or a regular, everyday one, who operates inside the envelope?

Here's a question: In life, are you a test pilot who *pushes* the envelope, or a regular, every day one, who operates *inside* the envelope?

It's not up to me to tell you which one you should be, but I will tell you that, while envelopes can be very safe, they are designed to hold things in. Things like vision, opportunity, possibilities. You know, the fun stuff.

But, be warned! If you decide to push the envelope, you may never return to your original dimensions.

Have a good flight.

Y
O
U
R

P
E
E
L
S

H
E
R
E

"86" YOUR FILTERS

Several years ago I was introduced to the word *paradigm* and to the concept itself. It's often considered an overused word which many avoid as a cliche, but I like it. To me, nothing fits the bill like *paradigm* when you want to describe the way each of us view our world.

Paradigms are mental filters we have created. And only information with which we have learned to be comfortable and successful is allowed to pass.

In *Executive Thinking*, Leslie Kossoff wrote:

> *As humans, we are not limited to seeing things*
> *in one particular way. We choose to see things*
> *in a way that is most familiar to us.*

What an unfortunate and limiting condition that is—to choose to only see the familiar. Do you do that? Do I? If we do, how hard does a new idea or concept have to work to crash through our filters? Too hard, I fear.

We are so proud of ourselves when we subscribe to a new way of thinking or behaving. How enlightened we are!

But how many less persistent, yet no less worthy and valuable ideas have we slammed the door on? That's a troubling thought, isn't it?!

For years I didn't like broccoli. Wouldn't let it through my "vegetable filter." Then one day, in a moment of temporary starvation, I ate some and found that my taste buds had evolved to where broccoli now was good. I had a new vegetable paradigm, and today, broccoli is my green vegetable of choice. Sadly, how many years of broccoli enjoyment did I miss?

Asparagus was next, then artichoke hearts. Can Brussels sprouts be far behind? My vegetable possibilities are now endless. (Except for cauliflower. Still working on that.)

How hard does a new idea or concept have to work to crash through your filters?

Next time you are introduced to a new thought, idea, concept, paradigm, or vegetable, before you "86" it, make sure that you aren't looking through an old, worn, outdated filter. It might be holding you back.

A whole new world of delicious, low-hanging green things might be waiting for you just for the picking: the leafy kind, and the dead President kind. And all you have to do is "86" your filters.

Hollandaise sauce, anyone?

YOUR SECOND WIND

Billy Joel is a pretty fair musician and singer, but he's a world-class songwriter. He and I were born on the same day, so perhaps that's why I like his words. One of my favorite Joel lyrics is from his song, "Second Wind."

You're not the only one who's made mistakes,
But they're the only things
that you can truly call your own.

We are not likely to learn much when we succeed because we think it's a result of our being so smart. Nobody wants to think about lessons when there's so much self-congratulating to do.

Every failure is also a discovery. You may have actually discovered something that no one else knows.

When we fail, we have more time to reflect on what happened because there's less celebrating. Use the time wisely. Don't wallow around feeling sorry for yourself. Claim your failures. Remember what Billy said about mistakes, "...they're the only thing that you can truly call your own."

Every failure is also a discovery. You may have

actually discovered something that no one else knows. All of the great minds were well acquainted with failure. There are so many examples of world-changing discoveries that resulted from perseverance in the face of bitter, demoralizing failures.

In one of my favorite books, *The Words Lincoln Lived By*, by my friend, Gene Griessman, I found this quote from Lincoln on adversity:

> *I find quite as much material for a lecture in those points wherein I have failed, as in those wherein I have been moderately successful.*

If you don't believe Billy and me, you have to believe Honest Abe. You learn more from your failures than from your successes.

I can't think of a better way to leave you than with the chorus to Billy's "Second Wind."

> *Don't forget your second wind.*
> *Sooner or later you'll feel*
> *that momentum kick in.*

CORE ENTREPRENEURIAL VALUES

I talk with a lot of budding entrepreneurs, and am constantly amazed at how many have not conducted anything close to a prudent amount of research as they start their businesses. And yet they often act as if they *must* get their business going *right now* or they will just pop.

This kind of impatience is dangerous.

I do my best to talk them down off the ledge. I walk the fine line between slowing them down a little and dousing their entrepreneurial fire. No use talking about due diligence, planning, or fundamentals. When would-be small business owners get that faraway look in their eyes, I try to get them to focus on the concept of passion. Not passion for being a business owner—passion for what the business *does*.

I believe it's critical to make the distinction because there will be times when you will hate being a business owner. Trust me on this one. When it all goes to hell in a handbasket, you will wish you were anything but the one on whom the buck stops.

But if you love *what* you do instead of *how* you do it— if you would rather be selling suits, fixing fenders, or baking bagels than anything else in the world, *that* passion will sustain you when all of the business stuff clouds up and rains on you.

My friend, Kelle Olwyler, co-author of *Paradoxical Thinking*, likes to talk about values. She helped me develop another way to define passion, which I call *Core Entrepreneurial Values* (CEV).

From now on, I will ask an impetuous entrepreneur, "What are your core entrepreneurial values? What is at the core of why you want to start this new business?"

If the answer is money, independence, status, etc., those are motivations, not values. At least not the kind of values that will get you through the week when you don't know how you are going to make payroll.

> ...*focus on the concept of passion. Not passion for being a business owner— passion for what the business does.*

But if the answer is suits, or fenders, or bagels—if you go to bed thinking about them, dream about them, and wake up thinking about them—well then, your CEV will not only allow you to deal with the cloudy days, but will actually help you grow on the rainy ones.

And if you can learn how to grow in the rain, think of

what you can do in the sun!

Now go spend an hour writing down your Core Entrepreneurial Values. Then send me a copy.

Y
O
U
R

P
E
E
L
S

H
E
R
E

THE WORLD ACCORDING TO
JIM BLASINGAME

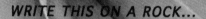

WRITE THIS ON A ROCK...

In life, are you a test pilot who pushes the envelope, or a regular, everyday one, who operates safely, inside the envelope?

SAILING THE ENTREPRENEURIAL SEAS

A friend with a good job once said to me, "It must be frightening being a small business owner. You know, not having a guaranteed paycheck, benefits, and all."

I told him he was right. Sometimes it scares the hell out of me. And then, remembering being downsized twice in 18 months, I hit him with this: "It's almost as frightening as when I was an employee."

I came across this jewel recently. I don't know who said it first, but I like it.

> *A ship in the harbor is safe—but that's not what ships were made for.*

Were you made for the safe harbor of employment? If so, God bless you! Because the world must have lots of loyal, productive employees. Send me your resume.

All of life is a risk. Raising anchor and setting sail merely introduces you to different kinds...

Or were you made to sail the entrepreneurial open seas? If so, God be with you! Because you're not part of a large fleet. You navigate by the stars of the marketplace, and the storms, reefs, and pirates of this ocean take no prisoners.

If you were made to sail and not to lie at anchor, you will not only know storms, reefs, and pirates, but you will also know what your ship is made of—perspectives not possible at anchor, and voyages others only dream of.

Remember, all of life is a risk. Raising anchor and setting sail merely introduces you to different kinds of risks from those found in a safe harbor.

Good sailing, mate.

Y
O
U
R

P
E
E
L
S

H
E
R
E

"I HAVE NOT YET BEGUN TO FIGHT"

During the Revolutionary War, John Paul Jones was one of the most colorful and effective Americans ever to stick his finger in King George's eye. Penetrating enemy waters off of northeast England aboard the ramshackle *Le Bonhomme Richard*, Jones and his men made the acquaintance of the British warship *Serapis*, escorting a convoy of merchant ships.

In the ensuing battle, out-shipped and out-gunned, the *Richard* was so badly damaged that J.P.J.'s chivalrous opponent offered to accept a surrender.

Think of it: A lone invader, 3,000 miles from a safe harbor, and he's attacked and virtually blasted out of the water by a member of the navy that created "the empire on which the sun never sets." Surrender would seem prudent, right? Discretion is the better part of valor—that sort of thing.

Fast forward into a new millennium. Another revolutionary, John Paul Entrepreneur, is under attack and being virtually blasted out of the marketplace by a member of a Big Box empire on which it *seems* the sun doesn't set. A lone operator, out-gunned by a force that can sell products cheaper than he can buy them, J.P.E.'s not-so-chivalrous opponent not only isn't offering to accept surrender, he's actually indifferent to J.P.E.'s existence. Surrender seems prudent anyway, right? Discretion is the better part of valor—that sort of thing.

In case history wasn't your strong suit in school, let me tell you what happened to our first revolutionary. John Paul Jones *did* lose his ship. Indeed, the *Richard* eventually sank that day, just as it seemed it would. But not only didn't Jones and his men surrender, they attacked. The American underdogs actually boarded and captured the Brit ship, and sailed it away as heroes, to fight another day.

John Paul Entrepreneur is under attack and being virtually blasted out of the marketplace by a member of a Big Box empire.

Back to the future: Our latter-day revolutionary is still pondering his options. Should he abandon company and surrender, or should he fight for his dream, against all odds? What would you do?

If you believe in your plan, recognize that you will never out-gun the Big Box Empires, and attack with your ability to deliver value to your customers in ways that the Empires can never replicate, you are ready to claim the battle cry and attitude of one of the greatest revolutionary heroes in history, John Paul Jones. For it was this hero who, when faced with seemingly insurmountable odds, looked the enemy in the eye and said,

"Surrender? Sir, I have not yet begun to fight!"

Y
O
U
R

P
E
E
L
S

H
E
R
E

_____

_____

_____

_____

_____

_____

THE WORLD ACCORDING TO
JIM BLASINGAME

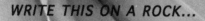

WRITE THIS ON A ROCK...

You can't cross the finish line halfway through the race. If you can't solve next week's problems today, don't let them trip you up today.

COLORING OUTSIDE THE LINES

Do you know what GAAP is? Generally Accepted Accounting Principles. These are accounting standards the financial auditing industry has established as a baseline for financial confidence in a company.

If you want your company to be accepted in the world of high finance, your accounting practices must conform to GAAP. The words are completely intuitive: generally accepted. Read: Color inside the lines. Poor accountants. If they want to be considered professionals, they can never color outside of the lines.

In the financial activity of our small businesses we should strive to understand and operate within GAAP. It's important to our long term success, and it keeps our financial partners happy. But beyond GAAP, I want you and your crayons outside the lines.

The marketplace is your canvas...

Sometimes I envy artists. When they need a new color they don't ask permission, or even care if anyone has ever put two particular colors together to make a new one—they just do it. And they keep mixing colors until they get just the right shade they are looking for.

What if we created an entirely new small business color palette? A new "marketing magenta," an innovative "strategic alliance alabaster," or a never-before-seen "prospecting periwinkle." (Sorry men, I know that's a girl color, but it does sound better than purple, don't you think?)

The Blasingame Mint has been coining again. Here's my newest term: NBIP. *Never Before Imagined Principles*.

From this day forward, when you're not being the person who has to make sure your company's accounting conforms to GAAP, spend some time thinking of yourself as the AIR—Artist In Residence. And your color palette is limited only by NBIP.

In the world of accounting, NBIP is not allowed. *Everywhere else* in the operation of your business, NBIP should be required.

The marketplace is your canvas—now start painting. And never mind those lines.

PRIORITY IS AN AGGRESSIVE WORD

Priority. Most of us use this word, and variations of it, quite often. It's a very useful word that is at the heart of accomplishment. Indeed, most accomplishments result only when we establish a chronological, practical, and strategic order of importance in, for example, components of a project, a field of endeavor, or our lives.

To help keep our priorities in perspective, I think it's important to understand that a priority is not passive—it's very aggressive. By definition, priority creates competition: Things compete in our minds for a place at the top of our priority list, seeking to control our time, attention, resources, and perhaps even our soul.

> *Things compete in our mind for a place at the top of our priority list, seeking to control our time, attention, resources, perhaps even our soul.*

What wins the priority competition in your life? Don't answer too quickly. This is an important question, but also a tricky one.

You probably didn't say "money," but let's tell the truth: How hard does money have to compete for a place at the top of your priority list? Take a look at what Adam Smith said about money in his 1776 landmark book, *The Wealth of Nations*:

> *It is not for its own sake that men desire money,*
> *but for the sake of what they can purchase with it.*

Money is important. In fact, Smith identifies money as one of the three most important inventions of mankind. But he also points out that money has no value in use, only value in exchange.

Money is only valuable to purchase things. Therefore, if money is your priority, then things are your priority, which begs the next question: How hard do things have to compete for a place at the top of your priority list?

Before cameras were idiot proof (fully automatic), I purchased a 35mm Nikon that had only one automatic feature, an auto shutter. The word *automatic* in a camera means something besides the idiot is calling the shots. In the case of my camera, when the shutter is set to automatic it takes its speed orders from the aperture setting on the lens, which is set manually. Nikon describes this operating relationship as *aperture priority*—the aperture calls the shots.

If Nikon were to describe your operating relationship,

what word would they put in front of *priority* as the thing that calls your shots? What is in control of your life? Here are some possibilities: Money, family, stuff, faith, (your idea here).

Let me help you. Write this down on a piece of paper and fill in the blanks.

The life of _____ operates by
(your name here)

_____ priority.
(your controlling interest here)

Then tape what you wrote on your morning mirror. Don't use glue. Remember, you may want to change your priorities.

THE WORLD ACCORDING TO
JIM BLASINGAME

WRITE THIS ON A ROCK...

The difference in entrepreneurs
is in how each decides when
to risk what is known
for what might be learned.

LEARNING SHOULD BE LIFELONG

Henry Ford is generally credited with being the creator of the assembly line. To meet the demand for his Model T automobiles, Mr. Ford knew that just hiring more people wouldn't be enough to mount the challenge of building Ford Motor Company; it would take technology. His technology was crude by our standards, but it did what technology does: *leveraged the productivity of human beings.*

During the year Ford's assembly line was first put in service, he wasn't just using technology, he was *creating* it. He was also turning 50.

How much have you looked into adopting technology to help you leverage the humans in your organization? Accounting and prospect management software, features-rich cell phones, networking your computers: The list is endless.

You can literally go from being a technology illiterate to being an application expert within weeks. But you do have to take that first step.

Some people don't embrace technology because they think they have gotten too far behind the curve. Hogwash! There is so much point-and-click technological capability these days that you can ramp up on any learning curve within a matter of days, if not hours. And besides, rapid changes in technology mean you can catch up with anyone by being prepared to fully adopt the next generation of capability that's usually never more than 90 days away. You can literally go from being a technology illiterate to being an application expert within weeks. But you do have to take that first step.

Some people whine that they are too old to learn all the new stuff. At 80 years old, the great Roman statesman, Cato (234-149 BC), began studying Greek. When asked why he would contemplate such a lengthy undertaking at such an advanced age, he replied, "This is the youngest age I have left."

Regardless of your age or level of technological proficiency, start learning and adopting the new technology. No excuses! Remember, it's the youngest age you have left.

BEING FIRST

He was a remarkable individual. In addition to being a composer and piano virtuoso, Ignace Jan Paderewski (1860-1941), was also a former Prime Minister of Poland.

Following a command performance on piano before Queen Victoria, she exclaimed, "Sir, you are a genius."

Alluding to all of the effort required to earn such adoration, Paderewski said, "Perhaps, your Majesty, but before that I was a drudge."

Webster: *drudge—a person who does hard, menial, tedious work.*

This story reminds me of a successful small business owner. People see the business doing well. The owner, as seen in the community, appears to be prosperous. Everything coming up roses, right? This must be a really smart person!

...first janitor, first truck driver, first receptionist, first inventory clerk, first accountant, and first salesperson—they're all the same person...

Here's the real story: Five, maybe ten years ago, the establishment associated with this entrepreneur may not have even existed. Going in and out of that business the first couple of years, you would have had the privilege of meeting its first janitor, first truck driver, first receptionist, first inventory clerk, first accountant, and first salesperson. No, you didn't make a bunch of new friends—just one. They're all the same person: Our *genius* small business owner, and first CEO.

Of course intelligence contributes to success in business. But I don't know any bright AND successful small business owners who don't know what the Prime Minister meant about being a drudge.

Next time you compliment a small business owner on his or her business' success, don't be surprised if the response sounds like, "Perhaps, your Majesty, but before that I was a drudge."

ATTITUDE IS EVERYTHING

In the world of small business, attitude is everything. Yes, I know, profit is essential and cash is king. I've been guilty of spouting all of those types of platitudes, however true, myself. But more than anything you can buy, sell, count, hold, or distribute, assuming what I call *The Small Business Success Attitude* is essential to entrepreneurial success. Here is The Small Business Success Attitude:

I accept that my small business will face challenges every day. As I begin my day, I will assume the attitude that, regardless of the number of challenges or the degree of difficulty, if my business is to survive, I must face each one. Therefore, I know that the only thing in question today is how well I will respond to challenges, and the future of my business may depend on the answer to that question.

The *I Ching* (pronounced *yee jing*) is an ancient book of wisdom, the origin of which predates the written word. In English, *I Ching* means "Book Of Change." I was inspired to write The Small Business Success Attitude from this passage in the *I Ching*:

*The event is not important, but the response
to the event is everything.*

The author of the *I Ching* was certainly an entrepreneur in the marketplace of ideas. Perhaps from as far back as 10,000 years ago he was proposing that it's not what happens to you in life that you should worry about, because there will always be something happening. When events happen change will also happen, and armed with the *I Ching* attitude, or The Small Business Success Attitude, you have an opportunity to influence change.

*...assume the attitude
that you must face
each challenge.*

Small business owners often feel that they don't have very much power. In the passage above, I believe the *I Ching* is telling us how to gain power and control in our lives. In The Small Business Success Attitude, I am absolutely telling you how to gain power and control in your business.

Accept the inevitable and ubiquitous challenges you will face in your small business, and get excited about the power you have to affect change simply by knowing that your "...response to the event is everything."

THREE-DIMENSIONAL ENTREPRENEURIALISM

Knowledge and creativity are the dynamic duo of entrepreneurialism. Armed with these two, small business owners deal with challenges and carve out new opportunities.

Sometimes we address challenges by using what we have learned, and then move on to the next one. That's the beauty of knowledge: It's always loaded up, ready to fire. It's also useful because we can share it by teaching others, which allows us to delegate, thereby leveraging ourselves.

But entrepreneurialism based solely on knowledge is two-dimensional. Most small business challenges require three-dimensional entrepreneurialism, which only occurs when creativity is blended with knowledge. Knowledge is critical to success in any endeavor. But in the world of entrepreneurs, creativity *must* flourish.

Entrepreneurs aren't limited by a dictionary, only by our knowledge and creativity.

The French novelist, Marcel Ayme, once said:

...from time-to-time, I find myself terribly limited by the words in the dictionary.

Because Ayme was a man of words, the dictionary held his knowledge, tools, and inventory. But sometimes, he lamented, it also held back his creativity.

I think Ayme was also telling us about his spirit. What else would cause him to imagine and yearn for something beyond what he knew to exist?

Entrepreneurs have Ayme's kind of spirit. As founders of business opportunities that haven't previously existed, our spirit drives us into uncharted territory. But we are more fortunate than Ayme: We aren't limited by a dictionary, only by our knowledge and creativity.

If you are feeling "terribly limited" by your entrepreneurial dictionary, perhaps you have been focusing too much on your knowledge and not enough on your creativity. Entrepreneurs use knowledge to identify and employ the "words" that are available to them. But rather than lamenting the ones they don't have, they use creativity to make the new ones they need.

It's a beautiful thing.

FAR FROM THE MADNESS OF CROWDS

In reading history we find that individuals have their whims and their peculiarities; their seasons of excitement and recklessness, when they care not what they do. We find that communities suddenly fix their minds upon one object, and go mad in its pursuit; that millions of people become simultaneously impressed with one delusion, and run after it, till their attention is caught by some new folly more captivating than the first.

Sound familiar? Like Dot-Com Mania? Actually, it's a passage from the 1841 classic, *Extraordinary Popular Delusions and the Madness of Crowds*, by Charles Mackay, republished in 1999 with a foreword by Sir John Templeton.

Mackay was talking about the psychology of crowds and their tendencies for creating mass mania. He had on his mind the Tulipomania (17th century), The Mississippi Scheme (18th century), and The South-Sea Bubble (18th century), but he could have been talking about Dot-Com Mania (late 20th - early 21st century).

When a fad comes along, like Beanie Babies, cigar bars,

or buying groceries online, there is opportunity to be had—no question. But typically only for an existing business which, along with its perennial products, adds the "new folly" product to its lines—not for a new business based solely *on* the "new folly."

There is tremendous pressure on small businesses to take advantage of the Internet: peer pressure, fear of missing an opportunity, fear of becoming uncompetitive, and yes, greed. Truth is, none of these are unworthy motivators. The problem comes when the manifestations of these pressures are misapplied in the form of mania.

> *There is tremendous pressure on small businesses to take advantage of the Internet.*

Please make sure you find and employ the technology and online applications your business needs to gain and maintain a competitive advantage. But make these applications complement your current business model, rather than getting caught up in some "new folly."

For if you should read Mr. Mackay's book on popular delusions and the madness of crowds, the last thing I want is for you to see yourself.

VISIONARY METALLURGY

Iron becomes steel, and therefore more useful, when most of the carbon, phosphorous, and sulfur are removed, and just the right amounts of chromium, manganese and nickel are added for hardening and durability. But it's an intense and disagreeable process that is pretty rough on the iron.

Entrepreneurial vision becomes clearer, and therefore, more likely to become reality, when myths and misinformation are removed, and just the right amount of research and critique are added for hardening and durability. But it's an intense and disagreeable process that is pretty rough on the entrepreneur.

Wise entrepreneurs know that the best plans are actually visionary alloys, forged in our mind from our vision and the critique of those on whom we road test our ideas. But one of the greatest challenges we face, as we transform our vision into reality, is in knowing which imperfections of our vision to remove and which parts of the new information and critique to put in.

...entrepreneurial vision is not passive: It's that rare, every-fiber-of-your-being kind of thing...

The reason this is such a challenge is because entrepreneurial vision is not passive: An entrepreneur's vision is that rare every-fiber-of-his-being kind of thing that has been hardening in the crucible of his mind, and anyone or anything which dares to disagree with that vision is often dismissed as being without vision.

During the alloying stage, the most common and unfortunate words to come out of an entrepreneur's mouth are, "Yes, but ... ," and "You don't understand, see ... ."

Here is some manganese wisdom from Mark Twain that I think will help in the forging process:

> *Keep away from people who try to belittle your*
> *ambitions. Small people always do that, but*
> *the really great make you feel that you, too,*
> *can somehow become great.*

If you want to forge the highest quality visionary alloy, you must include just the right amount of input from others—but it has to be the right "others." Don't blend your vision with the prattle of "small people." Find the "really great" and ask them to participate in helping you purify your visionary alloy, which will allow you to "become great."

TECHNOLOGY PEACE DIVIDEND

Unlike any other time in history, we can now actually leverage peace on earth through technology.

There is a significant increase in worldwide communication and business among small businesses and individuals (rather than just big governments and big businesses). I am convinced that we will—scratch that—*are* accruing a peace dividend from the connectivity opportunities made possible by the Internet, telecommunications, and other technologies.

As cold and impersonal as the word *technology* may seem, new global virtual relationships among ordinary folk are increasing exponentially, while existing ones are maturing and growing richer. These relationships are being created between people who have never actually met face-to-face, and may never meet.

...there are no geographical, political, or ideological boundaries in cyberspace...

With email, the Internet, and whatever new technological applications are on the way, it will become increasingly difficult to hate, or to be indifferent to, someone in another culture and country. Politicians (sometimes even dictators) can only wage war if they have the support of the people. When ordinary citizens and small business owners in America and China are communicating and doing business directly, why would they fight each other?

I am not a pacifist, nor am I a hopeless romantic, but perhaps a hopeful one. I know it will take time. But I believe at the dawn of the 22nd century, our great-grand-children will be living in peace worldwide, due in no small part to the fact that there are no geographical, political, or ideological boundaries in cyberspace between Beijing and Baltimore, Tehran and Terre Haute, or Havana and Hoboken.

But here is the challenge: It must start with us—you and me. Right now.

The world is changing in ways—and at a pace—that is unprecedented, and we aren't going to stop it. But we can make sure that the changes are good ones. The kind of changes that promote peace on earth and good will toward mankind.

Think about that next time you make a new friend in cyberspace.

INDEPENDENCE DAY IN AMERICA

Eleven score and five years ago...

> *...our fathers brought forth on this continent, a new nation, conceived in liberty and dedicated to the proposition that all men are created equal.*

Great words by a great statesman, President Abraham Lincoln, with adjustments in the chronology by a patriot, but not a statesman.

Here are some words from another great American, Thomas Jefferson, who penned one of the most famous and most important secular documents in history, the Declaration Of Independence.

> *We hold these truths to be self-evident, that all men are created equal, that they are endowed by their Creator with certain unalienable rights, that among these are Life, Liberty, and the pursuit of Happiness.*

I know you've heard these quotes before, and like me,

probably have memorized them. But I think they are beautiful, and seeing them in print and saying them out loud gets my patriotic juices flowing.

It's true, there have been lapses in America's delivery of some of the tenets in these passages. To be sure, America has had its share of failures.

But I like to think that America is a work-in-progress. That we are on a journey of understanding that has many stations where new things can be learned and wrongs can be righted. Along with the breakdowns and disappointments have been some great accomplishments and success stories that have made America and the world a better place.

No entrepreneurial soil is more fertile than in America...

Having the spirit and courage to write a declaration of independence is a pretty special thing. But fighting for its principles in the beginning, and defending them from within and without for over two centuries, is evidence of something extraordinary.

"Life, Liberty, and the pursuit of Happiness" have been important to small business. If you ask anyone anywhere on the planet where to go to start a small business and have the greatest chance to succeed, regardless of who you are or where you came from, the answer, without question, would be America.

Freedom to dream is found in other lands, as is freedom to pursue dreams. But no entrepreneurial soil is more fertile than in America, and it's largely because of those who had the *spirit* to create documents that include the passages quoted herein, the *will* to deliver them, and the *courage* to defend them.

Sound familiar? Small business owners around the world demonstrate *spirit*, *will*, and *courage* every day. Extraordinary. Very special.

God bless America's Founders and all who have helped to perpetuate the beacon of liberty that has shone so brightly around the world.

And God bless small business owners everywhere.

THE WORLD ACCORDING TO
JIM BLASINGAME

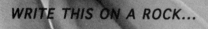

WRITE THIS ON A ROCK...

The success of your business is not so much subject to the challenges you face, as it is in how you respond to those challenges.

Y
O
U
R

P
E
E
L
S

H
E
R
E

SOURCES

Allen, Marc, *A Visionary Life*, New World Library, Novato, Calif., 1997.

------, *Visionary Business*, New World Library, Novato, Calif., 1997.

Bailey, Joseph, *The Speed Trap*, HarperCollins, New York, 1999.

Ballard, James, *What's the Rush*, Broadway Books, New York, 1999.

Carew, Jack, *The Mentor*, Donald I. Fine, New York, 1998.

Carter-Scott, Chérie, *If Life is a Game, These are the Rules*, Broadway Books, New York, 1998.

Chandler, Steve, *17 Lies That Are Holding You Back & the Truth That Will Set You Free*, Renaissance Books, Los Angeles, 2000.

------, *Reinventing Yourself*, Career Press, Franklin Lakes, NJ, 1998.

Condrill, Jo, *A Millennium Primer*, GoalMinds, Los Angeles, 1999.

Dauten, Dale, *The Max Strategy*, William Morrow, New York, 1996.

Dilenschneider, Robert, *Moses: CEO,* New Millennium Press, Beverly Hills, 2000.

Donovan, Jim, *This Is Your Life, Not a Dress Rehearsal*, Lahaska Publishing, Buckingham, Penn., 1999.

Eiseley, Loren, *The Star Thrower*, Harcourt, New York, 1979.

Feltenstein, Tom, *Uncommon Wisdom*, Lebhar-Friedman, New York, 1999.

Fletcher, Jerry and Olwyler, Kelle, *Paradoxical Thinking,* Berrett-Koehler, San Francisco, 1997.

Griessman, Eugene, *The Words Lincoln Lived By*, Simon & Schuster, New York, 1997.

Hurt, Floyd, *Rousing Creativity, Think New Now!*, Crisp, Menlo Park, Calif., 1999.

Jaffe, Azriela, *Create Your Own Luck*, Adams Media, Holbrook, Mass., 2000.

Jolles, Robert, *Customer Centered Selling,* The Free Press, New York, 1998.

Kossoff, Leslie, *Executive Thinking*, Davies-Black, Palo Alto, Calif., 1999.

Lorie, Peter, and Mascetti, Manuela Dunn (eds.), *The Quotable Spirit*, Castle, Edison, N.J., 1996.

Mackay, Charles, *Extraordinary Popular Delusions and the Madness of Crowds* (originally published by Richard Bentley, London, 1841), Templeton Foundation Press, Philadelphia, 1999.

McCann, Jim, *Stop and Sell the Roses: Lessons from Business & Life*, Ballantine Books, New York, 1998.

O'Donohue, John, *Anam Cara*, HarperCollins, New York, 1999.

Smith, Adam, *The Wealth of Nations* (originally published in Scotland, 1776), Random House, New York, 1994.

Trogden, William Least Heat-Moon, *Blue Highways*, Little, Brown & Company, Boston, 1999.

YOU ARE A MEMBER

...of The Small Business Advocate community if you own this book. If you ordered online, by phone, or by mail, that's all you have to do.

Otherwise, you can record your membership by sending an email or fax to the coordinates on Page 123, to receive advance notice of, and a member discount on, Jim's next book.

Another way to join our community is to subscribe to Jim's FREE electronic newsletter, either from the website, or by mentioning that you want to subscribe in your email or fax.

CONGRATULATIONS!

You are now connected to the thousands of entrepreneurs in Jim's worldwide listening and reading audience. Plus you're only one degree of separation away from the hundreds of members of The Small Business Advocate Brain Trust. Tune in to Jim's show on the radio or the Internet for a direct connection.

Welcome aboard.

CONCERNED ABOUT PRIVACY?

Don't worry, we are, too. We have a very simple and very STRICT privacy policy: Your information stays with us. ALWAYS!

ABOUT THE AUTHOR

Jim Blasingame is the creator and host of the nationally syndicated weekday Radio/Internet talk show, The Small Business Advocate, on the air since 1997. Jim has assembled a community of hundreds of small business experts he calls the Brain Trust, whom he interviews daily on his show.

Jim's web site, www.jbsba.com, is a leading-edge multimedia Internet resource. Jim is one of the pioneers in on-demand audio streaming, and was the first to offer small business audio content on the Internet in three formats: Live, Replay, and Archives.

In 2000, Jim was selected by *Fortune Small Business* magazine as one of the **Power 30**, the most influential people in America representing small business interests. Jim is a nominee for the SBA's Small Business Journalist Of The Year award for 2002.

In addition to being an owner and a consultant to small businesses, Jim also had significant tenures with the U.S. Army, Sears, and Xerox. He has conducted business at all levels of the marketplace across the United States, as well as some foreign markets. Jim is a professional speaker and trainer, a prolific writer on small business issues, and he is The Small Business Advocate.

WHEN HE'S NOT WORKING

...Jim is a Rotarian (past-president, 10 year perfect attendance), an ardent supporter of Chambers Of Commerce (25 year member and past-board member), and teaches an adult Sunday School class (14 years).

Jim's greatest successes are: a daughter who is a critical care RN, a son who is a police officer and sergeant in the U.S. Marine Reserves, and one grandson. (Jim has taken "obnoxious grandparent" to a new level.)

Jim is a licensed pilot with instrument and multi-engine ratings. He owns a set of golf clubs, plays the guitar for his own amazement, and aspires to be a gourmet chef.

JIM BLASINGAME

...is available to deliver high energy keynote addresses at your meetings and conferences.

Jim is a veteran business consultant specializing in CEO coaching. He helps small organizations compete with big ones, and big organizations understand and reach small ones through his "small business according to small business" approach. For more information, contact...

Small Business Network, Inc.
Toll Free 888-823-2366
Fax 256-760-0027
Email .... dsb@jbsba.com
Web site .... www.jbsba.com

SMALL BUSINESS
IS LIKE A
BUNCH OF BANANAS

...is an excellent and timeless merchandising gift for customers and clients. We will customize your copies of Jim's book with a gold label on the cover, with your organization's name printed on it, such as...

> **Compliments of**
> **ABC Consulting**

If you wish, Jim can autograph your copies. Plus we have other customizing options to offer, and will consider your ideas.

For quantity discount pricing, customizing and special fulfillment options, please contact SBN Books.

Toll Free 888-823-2366
Fax 256-760-0027
Email .... mail@sbnbooks.com

Use this contact information for single orders as well, or go to www.sbnbooks.com to order online.